Backyard Birds

A FIREFLY BOOK

Published by Firefly Books Ltd. 2018

First printing

Publisher Cataloging-in-Publication Data (U.S.)

Library of Congress Control Number: 2018941945

Library and Archives Canada Cataloguing in Publication

A CIP record for this title is available from Library and Archives Canada

Published in the United States by
Firefly Books (U.S.) Inc.
P.O. Box 1338, Ellicott Station
Buffalo, New York 14205

Published in Canada by
Firefly Books Ltd.
50 Staples Avenue, Unit 1
Richmond Hill, Ontario L4B 0A7

Printed in China

(Above) *Backyard Birds*, Robert Bateman, age 14

This title was produced by:
Madison Press Books
31 Adelaide Street East, PO Box 608
Toronto, Ontario, Canada M5C 2J8
madisonpressbooks.com

Canada ▪|▪|▪ We acknowledge the financial support
of the Government of Canada

Backyard Birds
An Introduction

Robert Bateman with Ian Coutts

Consultation by Nancy Kovacs

FIREFLY BOOKS

A FIREFLY BOOKS / MADISON PRESS BOOK

Birth of a Birder

Bob Bateman 1943

It started with a Black-capped Chickadee. I was eight years old; the place was a country lane north of Toronto, where I grew up. On that cold November day, something caught my eye. It was a lively little ball of fluff, hopping from twig to twig in a leafless hedge. I forgot about the cold as I watched the agile little bird with the black cap and white cheeks.

I don't know why, but from that moment I was hooked. Maybe it was the challenge of seeking something that didn't care about me but had its own exciting life. Soon I was spending hours in the ravine behind my house.

I inched through bushes with my ears and eyes wide open. It was an adventure — but a frustrating one, because I didn't know much about the birds I was seeing. And I had no books to help me.

I hope this book of some of my favorite birds will launch you on your own adventure. Of all wild creatures, birds are the most colorful and the easiest to see. You don't need to travel to distant jungles or faraway islands. They live in our backyards. If you just spend time watching and listening, you will discover them. You'll see their beautiful feathers and hear their amazing songs. You'll watch them feed in winter and build nests in spring. Birds are our neighbors. We should get to know them.

Black-capped Chickadee

Length: 5.25"/ 13 cm

Wingspan: 8" / 20 cm

Weight: 0.39 oz / 12 g

Voice: Common and familiar call is *chickadee-dee-dee-dee*

Food: Spiders, insects, seeds (especially sunflower seeds), and berries

Range: Northern U.S. and most of Canada

Habitat: Forests, thickets, groves, and residential areas

Mallards and Canada Geese

Male Mallards (opposite) are easy to identify because of their bright green heads. Females are streaky brown with a narrow, striking blue band on their wings.

While some ducks dive under the water to catch fish, Mallards prefer to eat plants. To reach the ones that grow on the bottom of rivers and ponds, they tip headfirst to nibble them. You will often see them "dabbling" this way, with their pointy rear ends poking out of the water.

Canada Geese are members of the same family as ducks. Like ducks, they have webbed feet for swimming and large bills to scoop up their food. Not long ago, it was rare to see a Canada Goose. Today, they are all over the continent and have been introduced to Europe and New Zealand. You will often hear geese overhead as they fly in their well-known "V" formation, honking loudly as they go.

Mallard

Length: 23" / 58 cm

Wingspan: 35" / 89 cm

Weight: 2.4 lbs / 1.1 kg

Voice: Males yeeb; females qweek or quack quack

Food: Mainly plant seeds taken from shallow water

Range: Most of continental U.S. and Alaska; Canada from Quebec west to the Pacific

Habitat: Any shallow fresh water

Canada Goose

Length: 25–43" / 63–109 cm

Voice: *Honk*

Food: Grasses and grains; along coasts, mollusks and small crustaceans

Range: Throughout North America

Habitat: Ponds, marshes, farmlands

Great Blue Heron

Length: 46"/ 117 cm

Wingspan: 72" / 183 cm

Weight: 5.3 lbs / 2.4 kg

Voice: A deep, croaking *frahnk, frahnk, frahnk*

Food: Amphibians, fish, insects, small mammals

Range: Across the U.S. and most of southern Canada

Habitat: Streams, rivers, lakes

Great Blue Herons and Belted Kingfishers

Walk along the shore of a lake, river, or marsh and you'll likely come across one of our largest water birds, the Great Blue Heron.

When it hunts, the Great Blue stays very still, staring down its long bill, its neck curved like an S. Seeing something, it snaps its neck like a whip — its head shoots out and it spears its victim with its bill. The heron usually hunts for frogs and little fish, but will grab a mouse or other small mammal. Keep watching, and you will see the heron's dinner slowly make its way down that long, slim throat.

The handsome Belted Kingfisher hunts for fish very differently. It perches in a tree or flies over the water, searching. Spotting a fish, it dives straight down, grasps the fish in its bill, then carries it to a nearby perch. It bangs the fish against a branch, then flips it into the air and swallows it headfirst.

Belted Kingfisher

Length: 13" / 33 cm

Voice: A long, loud, dry rattle

Food: Fish, amphibians, crustaceans, aquatic insects

Range: Throughout North America

Habitat: Streams, lakes, bays, coasts

Red-tailed Hawks and Great Horned Owls

Many birds eat nuts, seeds, and insects. But birds of prey feed on mice and rabbits, big fish, or even other birds. They boast strong feet called talons to grab their victims and hooked bills to tear at meat. The Red-tailed Hawk is one of the most common birds of prey. These birds like open fields, but also live in cities. You will often see them perched on fence posts or telephone poles from which they swoop down and grab their prey. If you are lucky, you may see them flying overhead. From below, you can identify them by their reddish, outspread tails. Other birds of prey include the Peregrine Falcon and the Bald Eagle.

Owls usually hunt at night. Great Horned Owls are named for the two tufts of feathers on their heads. These large owls hunt smaller birds, mice, and rats — even cats, chickens, and skunks. You may hear their loud "hoo-hoo-hoo" from the deep woods. They can be hard to spot, but if you notice a group of crows making a huge racket around a tree, they could be trying to chase an owl from their territory.

Great Horned Owl

Length: 22" / 56 cm

Voice: Deep, muffled *hoo, hoo-oo, hoo, hoo*

Food: Small mammals, skunks, cats

Range: Throughout North America

Habitat: Forests, woodlands, along streams, in open country

Red-tailed Hawk

Length: 19"/ 48 cm

Wingspan: 49" / 125 cm

Weight: 2.4 lbs / 1.1 kg

Voice: A hoarsely screamed *tsseee-arr*

Food: Small mammals such as rabbits, mice, and rats

Range: Most of the U.S. and Canada up to the Arctic

Habitat: Mixed country of pastures or fields with nearby trees; often perched along roads

Bird Senses

Birds are remarkable creatures. They live in the coldest parts of the Arctic and the hottest deserts. Some live most of their lives on the water. Others can fly enormous distances without landing. Here are some of the unique abilities and features that help birds survive.

Eyes

Most birds see much better than people. Some hunting birds, like eagles (right) and hawks, can see a mouse a mile away. Some birds are able to see a color our eyes cannot — ultraviolet. The Black-chinned Tanager from South America identifies its fellow tanagers by a patch of ultraviolet feathers on their backs.

Ears

Birds do not have ears like ours. Instead, they have coverts — special feathers that cover their ear openings. Some birds have very good hearing. The Barn Owl (left), for example, hunts in total darkness, but it can hear a mouse scurrying along the ground. Its ears can even tell it whether the mouse is headed left or right. Without ever spying its prey, it sweeps in and grabs it.

Voice

Birdsong can be beautiful, and birds communicate many things with their voices. A male's song will attract a mate, announce egg hatching, or let other birds know that this is his territory. Other sounds repel intruders or warn of predators.

Some birds, like the Mockingbird and Catbird, are accomplished mimics. These vocal tricksters can imitate many bird songs, including the high, whistled tones of the White-crowned Sparrow (right).

Brain

They may be bird-brained, but birds are not stupid. Black-capped Chickadees store nuts for the winter and remember where they put them. Others, like Blue Jays, can imitate other birds and even car alarms.

Crows may be the smartest of all birds. Some clever crows will drop nuts under the wheels of moving cars, then eat the nuts once the car has cracked the shells for them!

Feathers

Feathers are made of the same material as our fingernails. They're strong but light, help a bird fly, and keep it warm and dry. Their colors also help a bird attract a mate.

The Canada Goose (right) spends much of its time in water, but it doesn't get soaked. With its bill, it rubs special water-repellent oil from a gland at the base of its tail through its feathers. Without this oil, most waterfowl would get waterlogged and could not survive.

Mourning Dove

Length: 12"/31 cm

Wingspan: 18" / 46 cm

Weight: 4.2 oz / 119 g

Voice: *Cooah-coo-coo-coo*

Food: Grains, seeds, or small nuts

Range: Across the U.S. and southern Canada

Habitat: Farms, towns, open woods, scrub, and grasslands

Mourning Doves and Wild Turkeys

You can see Mourning Doves almost anywhere. This long-tailed bird is found in farmers' fields, forests, towns, and suburbs. Its name comes from its call, a mournful cooing sound. The Mourning Dove likes to feed on seeds that have fallen from backyard bird feeders. One of its most interesting features is that its wings whistle when it flies. Mourning Doves are game birds and can legally be hunted in many places. Some places protect them, however, so that they will not become extinct like the Passenger Pigeon.

The Wild Turkey is another game bird. It is closely related to the Domestic Turkey we eat at Thanksgiving. Not long ago, Wild Turkeys were nearly all gone because of overhunting and the loss of their forest habitats. But conservation efforts have helped save the Wild Turkey. It is now doing well and spreading across North America.

This male Turkey (below) is trying to impress a female by lifting up his tail feathers and fanning them out. He does this in the spring during mating season. His head and neck may also change from blue-gray to bright blue and red to attract a mate.

Wild Turkey

Length: 48" / 122 cm

Voice: Male *gobble;* female, sharp *tuk*

Food: Seeds, nuts, acorns, fruit, grains, some insects

Range: Much of U.S.; scattered in the West; southernmost Canada

Habitat: Open woods, forests, swamps, clearings

Ruby-throated Hummingbirds and Rufous Hummingbirds

When I was a young birder, the Ruby-throated Hummingbird was one of the first birds that I noticed. Who could ignore it? To see one buzzing about on a hot, still, summer day is unforgettable. Hummingbirds live mostly on the nectar of flowers, which they drink with their long bills. When they see a flower they like, such as the columbine (opposite), hummingbirds will zip right up to it. Then, hovering by beating their wings rapidly, they drink. They are great flyers. Not only can they hover, they can also back up and fly sideways — even upside down. No other bird can do that. They are also aggressive little birds. When not feeding, the bright green and red male Ruby-throat spends a lot of time chasing off other males.

The Ruby-throat is the only eastern hummingbird, but there are many hummingbirds in the West. The most common is the Rufous Hummingbird. This little reddish-brown bird is found from the Mexican border right up through British Columbia to southern Alaska.

Rufous Hummingbird

Length: 3.5" / 9 cm

Voice: High, chipped *tyuk*; sharp *buzz*

Food: Nectar, small insects, spiders

Range: Western North America, occasionally in the East in October–December

Habitat: Forests, brush, meadows

Ruby-throated Hummingbird

Length: 3.75"/ 10 cm

Wingspan: 4.5"/ 11 cm

Weight: 0.11 oz / 3.1 g

Voice: Chase call is a sharp, sputtering zeek idididid

Food: Flower nectar and fruit flies, gnats, mosquitoes, spiders, and caterpillars

Range: Eastern North America

Habitat: Gardens and the edges of woods

The Cycle of Family Life

Raising a family is the most important part of a bird's life. Birds have their babies in the spring and summer, when food is plentiful. Before winter, the chicks will be big enough to look after themselves.

Mating

In spring, the male bird claims a territory and seeks a mate. Some species, like hummingbirds, mate for only a short time. Swans, geese, loons (right), and others may mate for life. To attract a female, a male may sing or show off his bright feathers. Woodpeckers drum rapidly on hard surfaces with their bills as a display. Other birds, such as Prairie Chickens and Whooping Cranes, perform a dance.

Nest-building

Some nests are just a depression in the sand, while others are fancier. Cliff Swallows create little houses out of balls of clay. The Baltimore Oriole (left) makes a hanging nest to shelter its babies. Hummingbirds weave little cups of plant fuzz and spider web, and cover them with lichens.

Eggs

Most birds lay three to five eggs, but there are exceptions. Northern Gannets and Band-tailed Pigeons lay one egg, while Wood Ducks and Northern Bobwhites lay twelve to fourteen. Parents guard the nest closely. If they see an enemy, they will attack it or cry loudly. Get too close to a Killdeer nest and the mother will try to distract you by running away with one wing hanging as if broken. Many birds will abandon their nests if they are disturbed, so it is best to watch from a distance.

Newborn Birds

Most water birds, including ducks (below), are "precocial." This means they are covered with down when they hatch and can get around and feed themselves almost right away. They do not need much parental care. Most other birds, however, are born featherless, blind and helpless. When a parent approaches the nest, the babies poke their heads up, chirping to be fed (right).

Fledglings

When young birds are bigger and have feathers, they begin to hop out of the nest and perch nearby. They may need help to actually fly. The Osprey mother, for example, sits near the nest with a fish. Her hungry fledglings leap into the air, flapping their wings. Finally they fly over to get the fish.

By fall, almost all young birds are independent. The following spring, they will mate and start their own families.

Barn Swallows and Chimney Swifts

The thing I like best about Barn Swallows is that they're such fantastic flyers. You'll see a young one like this (opposite) fly right through a little crack in the wall of an old barn, circle around inside, and suddenly stop by flaring its tail. While hunting, Barn Swallows make long, diving swoops to catch their insect prey. They will even swoop down over a pond to take a drink of water.

The Chimney Swift also catches insects in flight, but it hunts at dawn and dusk rather than during the day. A cigar-shaped bird with short wings, the Chimney Swift doesn't swoop like a swallow. It beats its wings very fast, with one wing going up and the other going down at the same time. This gives it a slightly crazy look in the air.

Chimney Swifts' nests, like the one shown below, are also very unusual. They gather twigs and stick them directly to a wall in an old house or other sheltered place (yes, even a chimney) with their glue-like saliva.

Chimney Swift

Length: 5.25" / 13.5 cm

Voice: Loud, rapid twittering

Food: Insects, spiders

Range: Summers in eastern to mid-western U.S. and southern Canada; rare in southwestern U.S.

Habitat: Open sky over cities, towns

Barn Swallow

Length: 6.75"/ 17 cm

Wingspan: 15"/ 38 cm

Weight: 0.67 oz / 19 g

Voice: *Vit-vit*

Food: Small flying insects

Range: From Mexico across North America to the treeline

Habitat: Farms, fields, marshes, and other open lands; often perches on wires

Hairy Woodpeckers and Downy Woodpeckers

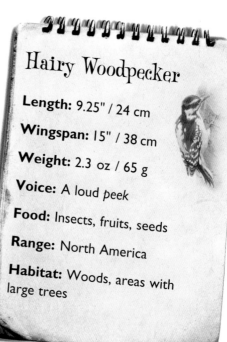

You hear a tap-tap-tapping in the trees. You follow the sound until you spot a woodpecker. It is black and white with a white back, so you know it is either a Hairy Woodpecker (opposite) or a Downy Woodpecker (below). But how can you tell which one you are seeing?

The red patch on the back of its head tells you the bird is male, since the females do not have any red. It has a long, rather heavy-looking bill and its tail feathers are white, with no markings. Its drumming is fast and long. Could these be clues?

Today is your lucky day, because a second woodpecker flies into a nearby tree. It is almost identical, but is clearly smaller, with a short bill. There are also some black markings on its white outer tail feathers. Its tapping is slower, lasts a shorter time, and is repeated often.

The mystery is solved: The first bird is the Hairy Woodpecker and the second is the Downy!

Hairy Woodpecker

Length: 9.25" / 24 cm

Wingspan: 15" / 38 cm

Weight: 2.3 oz / 65 g

Voice: A loud *peek*

Food: Insects, fruits, seeds

Range: North America

Habitat: Woods, areas with large trees

Downy Woodpecker

Length: 6.75" / 17 cm

Voice: A squeaky *pik pik pik pik*

Food: Insects, insect eggs, and grubs

Range: North America

Habitat: Forests, woodlots, willows, orchards, and shade trees

Dark-eyed Juncos and White-breasted Nuthatches

The little birds by the woodpile (opposite) are Dark-eyed Juncos. You will often see these slate-gray birds together like this in cold weather. They are busily hopping around on the ground, looking for seeds. You usually won't see them in summer. In the warm months, they live in the northern forests. In winter, they leave the woods to find food. Like many birds, they keep warm in below-freezing temperatures by fluffing up their feathers. And their bare legs and feet have special blood vessels that stop them from freezing.

The White-breasted Nuthatch is another bird you see more often in winter than summer. Like the Junco, it eats seeds. It likes to break them open first by pecking at them with its bill. You usually see White-breasted Nuthatches creeping down the trunks of trees looking for seeds and, in warmer weather, insects. They are agile little birds. It is not unusual to see them perched upside down on a swaying branch.

White-breasted Nuthatch

Length: 5.75" / 15 cm

Voice: Low, nasal, whistled *whi-whi-whi-whi*; also, a nasal *yank*

Food: Nuts, seeds, insects

Range: Across the U.S., most of southern Canada to the Maritimes

Habitat: Forests, woods, groves; visits feeders

Dark-eyed Junco

Length: 6.25" / 16 cm

Wingspan: 9.25" / 24 cm

Weight: 0.67 oz / 19 g

Voice: A very high, hard stip

Food: Insects, caterpillars, seeds

Range: North America

Habitat: In summer, forests, woods; in winter, open woods, brush, roadsides, and feeders

Migration

Migration is one of the most fascinating things about birds. We don't know for sure why birds first started moving north or south depending on the season, or why some birds migrate and others do not. The reasons probably have a lot to do with food. Many birds, like the Yellow-rumped Warbler (right) and House Wren (below), eat mostly insects. When winter comes, food becomes scarce, so the birds go to warmer places where there is more. Why don't birds stay in their winter homes all year round? It may be that the longer days of summer in northern climates give them more daylight to gather food for their babies.

Just before birds leave for the winter, you may see more of them than usual at feeders. Migrating is hard work, and they have to store up a lot of fat before they begin what can be a long journey. Swainson's Hawk flies all the way from the prairies of Canada and the United States to Argentina in South America — a distance of seven thousand miles or eleven thousand kilometers. You may spot an American Golden-Plover (below) feeding in a pasture or on the beach during its two-thousand-mile (three-thousand-kilometer) trip south. On the east coast, it can fly from Newfoundland to Brazil, over water the whole way — without stopping! But some birds don't go very far. The little Townsend's Solitaire only moves from high in the mountains to the valleys where it can find food.

How do birds know where to go? Some follow mountains and rivers. Others use the sun's location to navigate. Many birds that migrate by night use the stars and moon. Some, like the Bobolink (above), seem to have a built-in compass that guides them.

Early spring is exciting, as birds begin returning to their summer homes. Some may be coming to your region to nest. Others may be flying through to nesting grounds farther north. By late May, all over North America, the summer population is settled in to begin a new season of nesting and raising their young.

American Robins and Bluebirds

You can tell the male American Robin (opposite) by his bright-red breast. You'll see him hopping about the lawn, looking for worms. When he finds one, he quickly tugs it up before it can escape. The female Robin looks similar to the male, but her breast is a duller red. Unlike many birds, Robins aren't very afraid of people. They may even build their nests in people's porches. You can help by putting little flat pieces of wood up under the porch eaves for the parents to use as a nesting platform. The mother lays three or four eggs of a beautiful light blue that hatch in about two weeks. After that, the parents will be busy feeding their young. If you get too near the nest, the Robins will call "tuk-tuk" as a warning. It's best to leave them alone.

Like robins, bluebirds are members of the thrush family. We have three species of bluebird in North America: (below, from left to right) the Mountain, the Western, and the Eastern. Conservationists are worried about Western Bluebirds, whose numbers seem to be declining. Like the other bluebird species, they will readily nest in special nesting boxes provided by people in their yards, or on fence posts alongside fields.

Bluebird

Length: 6.75" / 17 cm

Voice: A low, whistled *pew* or *mew*

Food: Insects, berries

Range: (Mountain) Western North America; (Western) western U.S., southwestern Canada; (Eastern) east of the Rockies, southern Canada to Gulf States

Habitat: Open parklands, forests; near farms and orchards

American Robin

Length: 10" / 25 cm

Wingspan: 17" / 43 cm

Weight: 2.7 oz / 77 g

Voice: A series of low, whistled phrases, usually repeated two or three times

Food: Worms, insects, fruit, seeds

Range: All over North America

Habitat: Cities and towns, farmland and forests

Blue Jays and Gray Jays

Their bright blue, white, and black feathers and large size make Blue Jays (opposite) stand out. In the winter, you see them around feeders. They like to eat the sunflower seeds and cracked corn that fall to the ground. Jays are noisy, too. They have many calls, but the cry we associate with them most is "Jay! Jay!" They are great mimics, copying other birds, animals, even car horns! If Blue Jays think an owl or hawk wants to harm their young, a group of them will surround it and swoop down at its head, squawking loudly. When they see a squirrel or cat near their nest, both parents chase the intruder away.

Blue Jay

Length: 11"/ 28 cm

Wingspan: 16" / 41 cm

Weight: 3 oz / 85 g

Voice: Shrill, descending scream *jaaaay*

Food: Insects, nuts, and seeds

Range: Central and Eastern Canada and U.S.

Habitat: Oak and pine woods; towns and suburban gardens; feeders in winter

If you pull out a snack in the snowy northern woods and see a bold gray bird sailing straight toward you, you have found the Gray Jay. Known as the "camp robber," this graceful, charming bird may eat from your hand, or even steal your food when you're not looking. It hides food in trees for the winter by using its sticky saliva to glue the food in place.

Gray Jay

Length: 11.5" / 29 cm

Voice: Soft, clear *weeoo* and *weef weef weef weef*; husky *chuf-chuf-weef*

Food: Insects, nuts, and seeds

Range: Most of Canada and northwestern U.S., far northern New England

Habitat: Coniferous forests

Red-winged Blackbird

Length: 8.75" / 22 cm

Wingspan: 13" / 33 cm

Weight: 1.8 oz / 51 g

Voice: Gurgling trill *kon-ka-reee*

Food: Insects while breeding; fruit and grains the rest of the year

Range: North America

Habitat: Marshes and brushy swamps; wet areas near farmland

Red-winged Blackbirds and American Crows

The Red-winged Blackbird is one of the first birds to return to its breeding grounds each spring. He is black with red and yellow bars on each wing. Not long after he returns, he claims his territory. Preferring marshes and swamps, he flies from one cattail to another. You may see him perched there, wings spread, singing his distinctive song. "Stay away," he is telling the other males, "this is my territory."

The streaky brown female shows up a few weeks after the male and builds a nest in the reeds. Soon they are raising a family. The female stays close to the nest and is not seen as much as the male.

The American Crow is an enemy of the Red-winged Blackbird. This large, glossy black bird will try to steal the eggs from the Red-wing's nest. If the Red-wing spots a Crow, he will chase the larger bird, sometimes even grabbing on to the Crow's back and pecking at it furiously as it flies away.

American Crow

Length: 17.5" / 45 cm

Voice: A hoarse *carr* or *caaw*

Food: Any available food source, including garbage dumps and compost piles

Range: North America

Habitat: Open spaces for foraging and woods for nesting; urban areas

Northern Cardinals and Cedar Waxwings

The Northern Cardinal is one of our most familiar birds. The male is bright red and the female (opposite) is olive brown, with a little bit of red. Their crested heads are their prominent feature. When I was growing up in Toronto, Cardinals were rare. They lived in the American South, where they could find food all winter long. Today they are common residents, thanks to feeders they can visit in winter.

In summer, you can hear Cardinals singing high in the trees. Unlike most other birds, both male and female Cardinals sing.

The Cedar Waxwing is also crested. It is a glossy tan, with a black mask and a bright yellow tip on its tail. Waxwings love berries from junipers, European mountain ash, and other shrubs and trees. In fall, they gather in flocks to feed on berries to get ready for their long flight south.

Cedar Waxwing

Length: 7" / 18 cm
Voice: A high, thin zeee
Food: Fruit, sap, insects
Range: Throughout North America
Habitat: Open woodlands, fruit trees, orchards

Northern Cardinal

Length: 8.75"/ 22 cm

Wingspan: 12" / 31 cm

Weight: 1.6 oz / 45 g

Voice: A series of high, clear, sharp whistles: woit woit woit chew chew chew chew chew

Food: Insects, seeds, fruits, and grains

Range: Mexico; central and eastern U.S. and Canada

Habitat: The edges of woodlands and thickets; towns and suburban gardens

Attracting Birds to Your Backyard

Once you start looking, you will notice birds everywhere. They will be in a nearby park, in the trees on your street, and in your backyard. And you'll want to see even more. The good news is that it doesn't take much effort to get them to come to you.

A great way to attract birds is by putting out a bird feeder. If you don't have a backyard, you can put a feeder on a balcony, or even outside the window of your room. One filled with sunflower seeds and cracked corn will attract bigger birds like jays and cardinals (below). Filling it with smaller food, such as niger seeds, will draw juncos, nuthatches, and finches. My favorite thing is to get a small fireplace log, three or four inches (seven to ten centimeters) in diameter. I cut holes in it about the width of a bottle cap and an inch (2.5 centimeters) deep. I stuff the holes with suet mixed with oatmeal. Hang this up from one end and it will attract lots of birds, including woodpeckers (above).

Occasionally, someone's pet bird will escape its cage. If it is a seed-eater, your feeder will be very attractive. European Goldfinches, Rose-ringed Parakeets, Budgerigars (Budgies), Cockatoos, and Cockatiels have been spotted at backyard feeders, much to people's amazement.

Hummingbirds are always exciting to see, and you can put up a special feeder for them in your backyard. These feeders are bright red, the hummer's favorite color. Fill one with sugary water and watch the hummingbirds come. No red food coloring, though — it's not good for them. Make sure to clean out any little bugs and dirt that get inside. These can be harmful. You can also plant the bright flowers they like. Columbines, hollyhocks, and honeysuckle are three of their favorites.

Planting trees and shrubs like cedar and juniper also attracts birds. They can eat the berries, even in winter. In summer, shrubs and trees give birds places to hide and make nests.

In summer, a shallow birdbath will attract all kinds of birds. They will come to drink and splash around in it. Orioles, robins, starlings (right), and many other little birds like shallow birdbaths. Eagles, hawks, and owls like baths, too, but you probably won't get them to visit!

Baltimore Orioles and American Redstarts

With its black wings and brilliant orange body, the Baltimore Oriole is one of our most colorful birds. In springtime, the male will stand on the end of a branch, singing. He is staking out territory and looking for a mate. Until their eggs hatch, Oriole parents are not so easy to see. They spend much of their time high in the trees. The Baltimore Oriole is also famous for its nest. It uses bits of plants, string, and grass to build a sort of hanging pouch that swings from a high tree branch. The nest may look fragile as it sways in the wind, but it is very strong and in no danger of falling.

The American Redstart looks like a smaller Baltimore Oriole, but it is from a different family of birds known as wood warblers. These little birds live deep in the forest. You will not often see them. During migration, however, you may catch sight of one moving through woods, backyards, and ravines, flitting from branch to branch.

American Redstart

Length: 5" / 13 cm

Voice: High, rapid *tsee tsee tsee tsee tsee-o*

Food: Mostly insects; some seeds and berries

Range: Summers across Canada and eastern U.S.; rare in western U.S.

Habitat: Woodlands

Baltimore Oriole

Length: 8.75"/ 22 cm

Wingspan: 11.5" / 29 cm

Weight: 1.2 oz / 34 g

Voice: Short, clear, whistled pido o tewdi tewdi yewdi tew tidew

Food: Insects, spiders, fruit, and nectar

Range: Central and eastern Canada and U.S.

Habitat: Open woods; elms and shade trees in towns

Indigo Buntings and Rose-breasted Grosbeaks

The Indigo Bunting (opposite) and Rose-breasted Grosbeak are both finches. The finch family has the largest number of species in North America. Finches boast thick bills for cracking nuts and seeds. The male Indigo Bunting is a sparrow-size bird with brilliant, dark blue feathers. The female is brown and generally stays hidden. In spring, the male sings from trees along the edges of woods or in overgrown pastures. He is one of the few finches that sing while flying. He is at his deepest blue in the summer and molts in the fall, replacing old, worn feathers with new ones. In fall and winter, he looks brownish-blue.

Indigo Bunting

Length: 5.5" / 14 cm

Wingspan: 8" / 20 cm

Weight: 0.51 oz / 14.5 g

Voice: A high, sharp, whistled *swee, swee, chew, chew*

Food: Insects, berries, and seeds

Range: Eastern U.S. and Canada

Habitat: Roadsides and the edges of forests

The Rose-breasted Grosbeak is one of the finch family's largest members. It summers in forests and orchards, often visiting backyard feeders. It may even bring along its young once they have fledged. The Grosbeak can be hard to find high up in the trees, but its robin-like song can be heard ringing in the late-spring and early-summer woods.

Rose-breasted Grosbeak

Length: 8" / 20 cm

Voice: A slow, whistled warble

Food: Fruit, seeds, and insects

Range: Central and eastern Canada and U.S.

Habitat: Deciduous forests, orchards, and groves

American Goldfinches and House Finches

The male Goldfinch's bright yellow body and black wings contrast nicely with the dry, brown grasses and plants of late summer. (Like many birds, the female Goldfinch is duller in color than the male.) Goldfinches are country birds that love open fields. They have an unmistakable flying style, dipping as they cross the countryside. Their favorite foods are seeds from thistles, dandelions, and goldenrod — plants some think of as weeds. In winter, the brilliant yellow of the male is replaced by a duller olive brown.

The little reddish House Finch is originally from the western United States. About sixty years ago, people released some on Long Island near New York City. Since then, they have spread across the eastern United States and north into Canada. This House Finch (below) is perched on a yucca, a plant found in the desert. House Finches will build a nest anywhere that is convenient — in a flowerpot, even in another bird's nest. They love nuts and can often be seen eating them at feeders in the wintertime.

House Finch

Length: 6" / 15 cm

Voice: Whistled notes, often a long *veeeerrr*

Food: Vegetarian, including seeds and buds

Range: All of the U.S. and along the Canadian border

Habitat: Cities, suburbs, fields, desert brush

American Goldfinch

Length: 5" / 13 cm

Wingspan: 9" / 23 cm

Weight: 0.46 oz / 13 g

Voice: High, repeated phrases of *toWEE toWEE toWEE totweer tweer ti ti ti ti*

Food: Vegetarian, including seeds and buds

Range: North America

Habitat: Patches of weeds, thistles, and dandelions in fields, open woods, and roadsides

Spot the Sparrows

Some people think of all sparrows as "little brown birds" — hard to tell apart, so why bother to try? But when you know what to look for, these charming birds are pretty easy to identify.

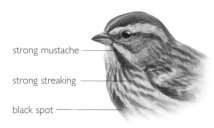

strong mustache

strong streaking

black spot

Song Sparrow

Look for the black spot on the Song Sparrow's chest, the brown and white streaks on its head, back, and breast, and a strong mustache running down its throat. Known for its singing, its most familiar song sounds like "Maids, maids, maids, hang up your teakettle-ettle-ettle!"

rusty crown

two-tone beak

rusty eye stripe

black spot

American Tree Sparrow

The Tree Sparrow has a black splotch on its gray chest, a red-brown cap, and a rusty stripe through its eye. Despite its name, it forages and nests on the ground. It summers in northern Canada and winters in much of the United States. Its song is a musical twitter.

rusty crown

black eye stripe

grayish breast

Chipping Sparrow

The Chipping Sparrow also has a red-brown cap, but no markings on its grayish breast. It has a black eye stripe and a broad white line over the eye. It makes a series of chipping sounds, sometimes running together to become almost a trill. It summers throughout most of North America.

White-throated Sparrow

Listen on early spring days for the White-throated Sparrow's call of "Old Sam Peabody, Peabody, Peabody," or "Oh, sweet Canada, Canada, Canada." It has a white throat, striped head, and yellow patch between its bill and eye, and can be found alongside roads, on forest edges, and in brush.

narrower white stripe

yellow lores (*area in front of eye*)

white throat

darker breast

White-crowned Sparrow

The White-crowned Sparrow has a broadly striped black and white head, gray throat, and yellowish-pink bill. It nests in northern and western Canada and summers across the southern United States. White-crowned and White-throated Sparrows often forage in the same places during migration.

broad white stripe

yellowish-pink bill

gray neck

House Sparrow

The House Sparrow is our most common sparrow, but it isn't even a native — or a sparrow! It is a Weaver Finch brought from Europe to North America in the 1870s. The male has a reddish-brown back and neck, a black throat, white cheeks, and gray crown. The female is more drab overall, with a plain throat and brown eye stripe. Boisterous and aggressive, it is often seen in cities, but even in the country it prefers to be near humans, frequently nesting in farm buildings.

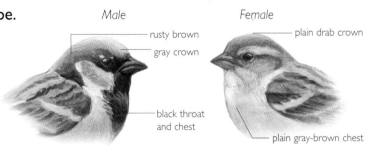

Male

rusty brown

gray crown

black throat and chest

Female

plain drab crown

plain gray-brown chest

Epilogue

Birds are fascinating. Just to see these colorful creatures flitting among the trees makes us want to learn more about them. We are so lucky that they are all around us — in our parks and yards. If you listen carefully, you may even hear bird songs in the background of your favorite television shows.

Birds are not just beautiful, though. They help us. Hummingbirds pollinate flowers. Swallows and swifts eat insects. Owls — like the Screech Owl (below) — and hawks feed on mice and other rodents that eat farmers' crops.

Sometimes, unfortunately, we do things that harm birds. All over the world, the forests where many birds make their homes are being cut down. Office buildings leave lights on all night, which dazzles migrating birds. They often fly into the buildings and are injured or killed. Chemicals that may harm birds are sprayed on fields to control insects and weeds. People cut down trees in their yards without replacing them and use sprays to control weeds and insects in their gardens.

We can help birds. For example, not long ago, a chemical called DDT was used to kill insects. Birds ate both the insects and the mammals that fed on them. The DDT got into their bodies and weakened the shells of the eggs they laid. Soon, such beautiful birds as the Bald Eagle and the Peregrine Falcon (opposite, top) were in danger of dying out. Fortunately, people saw what was happening and DDT was banned. After a few years, the numbers of eagles and falcons began to grow again.

There are many other ways we can help birds. In the spring and fall, we can turn out the lights in tall buildings. We can make sure that at least some of the forests and other areas where birds live and nest are preserved. And we can try to avoid using sprays and poisons on our lawns and gardens. Just pulling up weeds by hand could save countless birds. And, of course, we can plant the shrubs and flowers that provide food for them.

A little effort can make a huge difference. This is the birds' world, too. Let us take care to share it with them.

Glossary

Bill: The bird's "mouth," made of bone and other, more flexible materials. Depending on the bird and its diet, the bill is adapted to crushing seeds and nuts, grasping insects, sipping nectar, and so on.

Call: Sound, usually short and used for direct communication, such as to alert others to danger, to locate others of the same species, and to keep the flock together. Compare to *song*.

Conservation / Conservationist: The act of working to preserve the natural world. Conservationists can be anyone who studies, protects, or helps nature — from scientists to regular nature-lovers.

Crest: Slightly longer feathers on top of the head. Raised, they form a sort of peak. Crested birds include Cardinals, Blue Jays, and Cedar Waxwings.

Family: A scientific term for a large grouping of birds (or other life forms) with similar characteristics. The family contains smaller sub-groups called genus, which in turn contain different *species*.

Fledgling: A young bird who is ready to leave the nest, having developed flight feathers.

Habitat: Where a bird lives and raises its family.

Lore: The area between the eye and the *bill*.

Primaries: The outer wing feathers.

Range: The geographical area where a bird is likely to be seen. This includes winter and summer ranges and migration routes.

Secondaries: The wing feathers closest to the body.

Song: A more complex sound than the *call*, and usually learned. The song announces the bird's territory and can have many variations. Some birds have only one song, some several.

Species: Birds of the same type. These are the individual birds that we identify, like the Northern Cardinal and House Finch.

Talons: The very sharp "toenails" of birds that allow them to grasp their prey and carry it off.

Wingspan: The measurement of a bird from wingtip to wingtip.

Recommended Reading

Bird by David Burnie (Dorling Kindersley). Includes illustrations and information on the evolution, make-up, and behavior of birds.

Birdwise by Pamela M. Hickman, illustrated by Judie Shore (Kids Can Press). Activities include bird feeding, observation, and building bird houses.

Peterson First Guide to Birds of North America by Roger Tory Peterson (Houghton Mifflin). A junior version of the famous field guide, incorporating Peterson's system of using field marks for identification.

Web Site

Cornell Lab of Ornithology | www.birds.cornell.edu Includes a field guide, complete with bird calls.

Acknowledgments

The authors and Madison Press Books would like to thank Alex Fischer for her good cheer, clear and logical thinking, and most capable help throughout the process; Teresa Rigg of Backyard Heritage Discoveries for her helpful consultation; and Adrienne Fine-Furneaux for her work on the original research for this project.

Ian Coutts is an award-winning editor who has produced many internationally acclaimed, bestselling books throughout his long career. He is also an accomplished writer whose articles have appeared in such magazines as *Canadian Business*, *Toronto Life*, and *Canadian Geographic*.

Produced by

MADISON PRESS BOOKS
Toronto, Canada
www.madisonpressbooks.com

Project Editor: Nancy Kovacs
Executive Editor: Imoinda Romain
Editorial Assistance: Shima Aoki, Sandra L. Hall
Editorial Director: Wanda Nowakowska

Designer: Diana Sullada
Production Manager: Sandra L. Hall

Publisher: Oliver Salzmann

Printed in China